CLEVER
CARD
TRICKS

CLEVER CARD TRICKS

BOB LONGE

Main Street
A division of Sterling Publishing Co., Inc.
New York

10 9 8 7 6 5 4 3

Published by Sterling Publishing Co., Inc.
387 Park Avenue South, New York, NY 10016

This book is comprised of material from
the following Sterling Publishing Co., Inc. title:
Clever Card Tricks for the Hopelessly Clumsy © 2005
by Sterling Publishing Co., Inc.

Design by StarGraphics Studio

Printed in China

Sterling ISBN 1-4027-3137-X

For information about custom editions, special sales, premium and
corporate purchases, please contact Sterling Special Sales
Department at 800-805-5489 or specialsales@sterlingpub.com.

TABLE OF CONTENTS

CLEVER CARD TRICKS

CLEVER CARD TRICKS

INTRODUCTION

An argument can be made that almost every calling requires some amount of selling. It's certainly true of such diverse occupations as teaching, medicine, journalism, and law. And it's especially true of the performance of magic. The tricks are your product; the performance is selling.

A sales representative doesn't simply run the vacuum cleaner and expect a sale; he explains the benefits, indicates how much easier life will be, and paints a picture of total cleanliness accomplished with ease. And with magic, you don't just perform a trick and hope for the best: You must sell the trick. Some magicians, particularly stage performers, accomplish this with props, music, costumes, and such. Even so, in most instances the principal selling tool is the voice.

This is certainly true of card tricks. Apart from the deck itself, what other tools do you have? So you should use your voice cleverly and thoughtfully. What are you trying to sell? Yourself, of course. The group should feel that you're a good person. If you are, this should be an easy sell. So let's not worry about that. Basically, then, you're trying to sell the spectators on the validity of the trick you're doing. In other words, you're trying to fool them. And, at the same time, you want to entertain them. Your patter, your demeanor, your entire presentation should be aimed at this dual goal.

So try to develop patter for each trick. Give it a lot of thought. Present a story that's either serious or amusing, but is always interesting. Perhaps include an anecdote or two. (If you tell a joke and people laugh, that's a joke. If you tell a joke and nobody laughs, that's an illustrative anecdote.) You can orally create an atmosphere of mystery, recount a tale that will misdirect the attention of the group, or make a series of silly remarks that evoke laughter. The possibilities are endless.

As you practice a trick, be sure to include the patter. Thus your patter will improve as you perfect the mechanics, and you'll end up with a perfectly integrated and entertaining trick.

In this book you'll find a fascinating collection of card tricks that especially lend themselves to patter, for you're involved in all sorts of mental magic: prediction, strange coincidence, telepathy, feats of the conscious mind, and a number of hilarious mental tricks. Patter themes should readily spring to mind. If they don't, however, I offer patter suggestions for almost every trick.

When you decide to do mental magic with cards, you must decide whether you're going to be serious about it or not. Are you going to purport that you have superior mental powers? I prefer to be just as baffled as the rest of the group, taking the attitude, "I don't know why it works; it just does." I figure that I'm just doing card tricks; why would I want to pretend that I have some sort of mysterious access to the ultimate powers of the universe?

A deck of cards is ideal for performing mental magic because so much variety is possible. In fact, using some of the tricks presented here, you can do an entire show of mental magic. Or—my preference—you can include several as a part of your regular program.

If you prefer not to do mental magic, you may perform many of these items as simply mystifying card tricks. The only difference is the patter.

I'm very proud of this collection, and I'm sure you'll find many tricks that you'll enjoy performing.

MOVES & MANEUVERS

Preposterous Patter

Here we have some patter lines that many find funny. Some are original, but most have been concocted by others, and are quite ancient. Obviously, a joke isn't old to someone who hasn't heard it before, so you may find some of these useful.

But that is not my main purpose in presenting them to you. I hope that you'll observe the sort of lines that have found success. As with all humor, you'll find here the unexpected, the well-turned phrase, or the just-plain-silly. Perhaps some of these will give you some ideas on how to develop lines of your own to use with your tricks. In all of the tricks presented here, you will find patter suggestions that may inspire you to devise original comical lines to enhance your performance.

On the other hand, depending on your nature, you may decide to make a more serious presentation. Regardless, here are the lines, most of which are very familiar to experienced magicians.

1 Would you like to see a card trick? All right, then I'll have to get out my trick cards. I'm kidding. This is an ordinary deck of marked cards. Yes, they're marked. See the marks? This is a queen of spades. This is a 7 of hearts. This is a 5 of clubs. They're all marked."

2 "Take a card, any card . . ." The spectator does; ". . . except that one."

3 "We have here an ordinary deck of 57 cards."

4 Point up one sleeve. "Nothing here." Point up the other sleeve. "Nothing here." Point to your head. "And very little here."

5 "I believe your card is a cherry-colored card."
"No, it isn't."
"You've never heard of black cherries?"

6 "Your card is a licorice-colored card."
"No, it isn't."
"You've never heard of red licorice?"

7 "Do you know one card from the other?"
"Sure."
"Okay. Name one card. Come on . . . you can do it."
"6 of spades."
"Excellent. Now for something really tough. What's the other?"
"Jack of spades."
"Right! You do know one card from the other. Terrific job!"

8 "I am the most amazed person when one of my experiments happens to work. The magical result just astonishes me. When I do this stunt, however, I seldom have to worry about that."

9   With the right spectator, you might even be moderately insulting: "Hold out your hand, please. . . No, the clean one. Just kidding. Heck, my hands are almost as dirty as yours."

10   "Take a card. Now show it to your friends. This shouldn't take long."

11   "This is the first time I've ever made that mistake. . . again."

12   "I can't believe it! This entire deck of cards is printed upside down. Of course it's kind of hard to tell."

Control

Every magician who does card tricks must have some way of controlling a card after it has been chosen. Most methods require considerable skill. Here's one that's very easy.

Simplicity Itself

In some instances, this control works best. For example, you might want to bring the chosen card to a fairly high number from the top. This would do perfectly, as I'll explain.

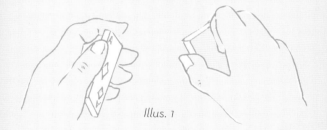

Illus. 1

Before the spectator chooses a card, sneak a peek at the bottom card of the deck. You can do this as you separate the deck in two, preparing to do a riffle shuffle (Illus. 1). Then, when you shuffle, keep the card on the bottom. Easier yet, look at the bottom card as you tap the side of the deck on the table, apparently evening up the cards (Illus. 2).

So you know the bottom card of the deck. Fan out the deck, and a spectator selects a card. Close up the deck. From the top of the deck, lift off a small packet and drop

Illus. 2

it onto the table. Lift off another small packet and drop it on top of the first one. After dropping several packets like this, say to the spectator, "Put your card here whenever you want." After you drop one of your packets, he places his card on top. You put the rest of the deck on top of it. Even up the cards and pick them up. The card that you peeked at is now above the chosen card.

Start fanning through the cards, their faces toward yourself. Mutter something about, "This is going to be really hard." Fan off several cards. Cut them to the rear of the deck. Fan off several more. Again, cut them to the rear. You're establishing a pattern so that it won't seem so odd when you finally cut the chosen card to a key position.

Let's say you simply want the card available on top of the deck. Continue fanning groups of cards and placing them at the rear until you see that you'll soon arrive at the key card. The card on the near side of the key card is the one chosen by the spectator (Illus. 3). Cut the cards so

Illus. 3

Illus. 4

that the key card becomes the top card of the deck (Illus. 4). Just below it, of course, is the chosen card. Turn the deck face down.

"I can't seem to find your card." Turn over the top card of the deck (the key card). "This isn't it, is it?" No. Turn the card over and stick it into the middle of the deck. Turn the deck face up. "How about this one?" No. Take the bottom card and stick it into the middle of the deck. Turn the deck face down. The chosen card is at your disposal on top of the deck.

Suppose, for purposes of a specific trick, you want the chosen card to be tenth from the top. Again you start by fanning off small groups and cutting them to the rear of the deck. When you get to the chosen card, you start counting to yourself. You count the chosen card as "One." Count the next card as "Two." Cut the cards so that the card at "Ten" becomes the top card. The chosen card is now tenth from the top.

False Cuts

An efficient false cut should be done casually, just as a genuine cut would be performed. Often magicians manipulate the cards back and forth between their hands, rapidly shift piles here and there, and finally end up with a single pile. Naturally, spectators don't know exactly what happened, but they sure as heck know that *something phony was done*. This is not always bad; sometimes it's alright to show that you're skillful. But many of us prefer to keep our skills—however minimal—secret. I recommend this.

Just a Casual Cut

Hold the deck in your left hand. With your right hand, lift off the top portion of the deck and place it face down onto the table. Make some casual remark. At the same time, without looking at the card, take the rest of the deck with your right hand. Place this pile to the right of those on the table.

Continue commenting. Glance down at the cards on the table. Pick up the pile on the right and place it on top of those on the left. Pick up the combined pile.

The cards retain their original order.

And Another

With the left hand, take the bottom portion of the deck. The left hand should be palm down, and the packet should be grasped with the second finger at the far end, the first finger on top, and the thumb at the near end. The top portion of the deck is retained in your right hand

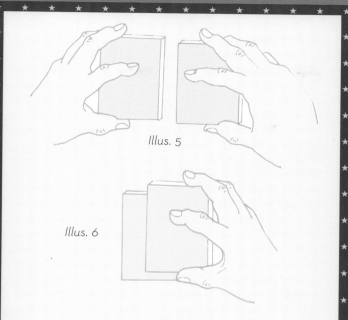

Illus. 5

Illus. 6

(Illus. 5). Gesture with the left hand as you make a comment. At the same time, drop your right hand somewhat, so that it becomes lower than the left hand.

Place the left-hand portion onto the table. Put the right-hand portion on top of it (Illus. 6). Pick up the entire deck with the right hand.

The cards are back in order.

Roll-Up Cut

I designed this cut specifically for the gambling trick "Really Wild," which appears in my book *World's Greatest Card Tricks*. There is no sleight of hand, and the deck is kept in order.

Since the cut does not appear ordinary, it can work well if you just give it a fancy name. For instance, you might say, "I'll just give the cards my 'inside-outside over-and-out cut.'" Or, "Here's my famous 'whoop-dee-doo and row-dee-dow cut.'" Actually, you can give it any extravagant name; I generally call it something different every time.

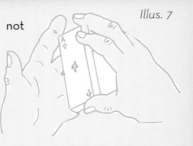

Illus. 7

Hold the deck in the dealing position in your left hand. With your left thumb, flip the deck face up. If the move is too difficult, simply grip the ends of the deck between the right fingers and thumb, and turn it over (Illus. 7).

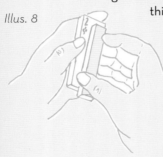

Illus. 8

With your right thumb, grip about a quarter of the face-up deck on the left side (Illus. 8). Lift this packet, pivoting it to the right, as though opening a book from the back (Illus. 9). Let the packet fall face

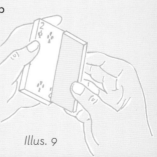

Illus. 9

Illus. 10

down onto your right hand. Place it face down to your left.

Flip the rest of the deck over with your left thumb so that the cards are now face down. As before, if this is too difficult, just turn the cards face down with your right hand.

With your right thumb, lift about a third of the face-down cards on the left side. Pivot these over, as before (as though opening a book from the back). Let the packet fall face up onto your right hand. Set the packet onto the table a few inches to the right of the first packet.

Again, flip the rest of the deck over with your left thumb, or turn it face up with your right hand. With your right thumb, pivot off about half of the cards and set them face down on the table to the right of the other two packets.

Remaining in your left hand is a packet of face-up cards. Take the packet into your right hand and set it face up to the right of the others. Pause, saying, "Now comes the hard part."

With your right hand, grasp the right side of the packet you just placed down. Turn this packet over on top of the packet to its left, as though closing the back portion of a book (Illus. 10). In the same way, turn the combined packet over and place it on the packet to its left. Once more, turn the combined packet over and place it on the packet to its left—the first packet you placed down.

Even up the cards. The deck is face down and in the precise order it was at the beginning.

If you follow the instruction with a deck of cards, it will seem that the cards can't possibly be in their original order. It just doesn't seem logical. Maybe I should have called it the "illogical cut."

Note

When lifting off the packets to place them onto the table, you may prefer to grasp them at the ends with the palm down right hand, fingers at the outer end and thumb at the inner end. As with the other method, you pivot the packet in an arc to the right, as though opening a book from the back. Then place the packet onto the table.

Milking the Cards

This is actually a fairly simple procedure with a small packet of cards. The idea is to slide off the top and bottom cards together and place the two together onto the table. Again, you slide off the top and bottom cards together and place these two on top of the first two. You continue like this until the pile is exhausted. The move is important in quite a few tricks.

Illus. 11

Let's get more specific. Hold a packet of cards from above in your palm-down left hand, thumb at the inner end, first finger resting loosely on top, and the other fingers at the outer end (Illus. 11). Your palm-up right hand lightly grips the top and bottom cards, thumb on top and fingers on the bottom. The right hand pulls the top and bottom cards to the right until they clear the packet (Illus. 12).

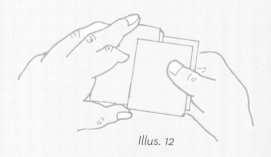

Illus. 12

The two cards are set onto the table. Draw off two more cards, dropping them on top of the first two. Continue until all the cards are in a pile on the table.

The Up-and-Down Shuffle

Anytime you perform this maneuver, you refer to it as a shuffle. Actually, it is not. It's a subtle method of rearranging the cards to your advantage. Usually, it is performed with a packet of cards—somewhere between ten and 25.

Start by holding the packet in the left hand in the dealing position. Push off the top card with your left thumb and take it with your right hand. Push off the next card with your left thumb. Move your right hand forward (away from you) a bit. Take this second card below the first card in your right hand. This second card should be two inches or so below the first card.

Move the cards in your right hand back toward you. Push off a third card with your left thumb. Take it below the first two cards so that it is even with the first card you drew off.

Move the cards in your right hand back toward you. Push off a fourth card with your left thumb. This card goes

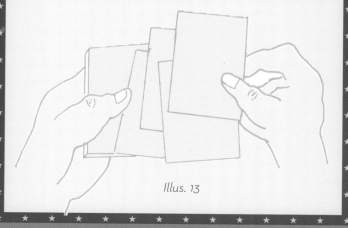

Illus. 13

on top of the others and is even with the second card you drew off (Illus. 13).

Illus. 14

Continue alternating like this until the packet is exhausted. Hold the upper group with your left hand as, with your right hand, you strip out the lower group from the others (Illus. 14). This group goes on top of the cards remaining in your left hand.

Notes

1 Depending on the trick, in the first move of the shuffle you may move the top card *down* or toward you, the next card up, the next card down, and so forth.

2 Depending on the trick, when you strip out the lower group (the cards nearest you), these will sometimes go *below* the cards you hold in your left hand.

3 Speed is not needed for this maneuver. If you take your time, you can do it quite easily.

What If Things Go Wrong?

You have the wrong card! For some inexplicable reason, the trick simply didn't work.

There are two cardinal rules: (1) Under no conditions try the trick again. (2) Don't blame the spectators.

You failed; accept it. Why did you fail? The possibilities are unlimited. Try one of these excuses, for instance:

"Just what I thought, the deck was too slippery."

"Well, the score is now one to nothing, your favor."

"What was your card?" She names it. "Just as I suspected. That's my 'bad luck' card."

"I'm not surprised. That trick never works. Let's try one that does."

"You have to admit one thing: If that worked, it would have been one heck of a great trick."

"It's my fault, really. I washed my hands this morning and now I can't do a thing with them."

"Gee! And only a few minutes ago, that used to be my favorite card trick."

I'm sure you can think of dozens of other silly excuses. The point is: Say something somewhat amusing and then get on with it; show another trick—preferably one that you're sure will work. Most will forget that you ever goofed up. And many will think it's all part of the show.

Above all, don't let it bother you. Remain composed as you proceed with your tricks. The old show-biz saying applies here: "Don't let them see you sweat."

HIDE & SEEK

Prints of Magic

Walter Gibson invented the main idea; I've combined it with a wonderful old trick.

You must know the name of the top card. A good way is to sneak a peek at the bottom card and, in an overhand shuffle, bring that bottom card to the top of the deck. Ask Henry to think of any number from one to 20, and to deal off that many cards into a pile on the table.

"Now," you tell Henry, "cut the remainder of the deck into two piles." After he does so, ask him to shuffle one of the two piles. Then he is to shuffle the other pile. Finally, point to the pile he first dealt off. "Please pick up those cards and hold them facing you so that you can see the bottom card but I can't. Remember that bottom card. Now, if you don't mind, just put your thumb print on the face of that card, right around the middle."

Pick up one of the other two piles and show Henry exactly how to affix his thumb print (Illus. 15). Say, "I'll turn away while you put your thumb print on the face of your card." Turn away for a moment and give these instructions: "Now shuffle that pile. Then put it

Illus. 15

together with the other piles and give the entire deck a shuffle." The card he "chose" is, of course, the card you originally peeked at.

Turn back and take the pack from Henry. Turn the top card face up and ask Henry to put his right thumb print on the face of that card. (If it happens that the top card is the one he chose, take a bow and *quit!*) Stare at the card, ostensibly studying the thumb print. "Very interesting. Should be easy to identify."

Set the card face up on the table. Turn the deck face up and begin spreading the cards out, glancing back and forth from the deck to the thumb-printed card as you try to find a match. Act this out, pausing here and there to study a possibility. It works well to go past the chosen card and, after spreading out several more, go back to it. Pick it up and compare it closely with the other card. "An exact match!" you declare. "This must be your card."

The Fooler

I call this trick The Fooler because magician Wally Wilson completely fooled me with this one. The secret is extremely subtle.

Ask Kevin to shuffle the deck thoroughly. "Now please think of a number from five to 15, and deal that many cards into a face-up pile." Start to turn away, but before your back is turned, catch a glimpse of the first card Kevin deals. That first card is your key card. That's it! You're all done with the sneaky portion of the trick.

"Look at the last card you dealt. That's your chosen card. In other words, your card is the one that's at your chosen number. Now cut off a pile from the top of the deck and set it on the table. Pick up the cards you dealt off, turn them face down, and place them on top of the pile in your hands. Put the pile you cut off on top of all."

Turn back to the audience. "There's no doubt now that your chosen card is buried in the middle of the deck where I can't possibly find it." Have Kevin give the deck a few complete cuts.

Take the deck and fan the cards face up before you, staring at one and then another. No luck. Shake your head. "I can't seem to get a picture of your card. Maybe this will help. . . . What was the number you thought of?" Suppose Kevin tells you 13. Still puzzled, you fan back and forth through the face-up cards. When you spot your key card, start with that card and count 13 cards towards the face of the deck. The thirteenth one is the selected card.

Tentatively remove the card and place it face down on the table. "Maybe this is it. What was your card?" Success!

Lucky Card Location

The spectator seems to make all the choices, yet you end up finding the chosen card. F. J. Baker had the original trick, which required a blank card. Since I seldom have one, I changed the handling slightly.

You must have a complete 52-card deck. Have Leonard shuffle the deck. Take the cards back, saying, "I have to find my lucky card. If all goes well, it will help with our next experiment." Fan through the cards with faces towards you. You must count to the twenty-fifth card. It will help allay spectator suspicion if you count the cards in groups of three. (Separate the cards after you count off 25.) The twenty-sixth card from the bottom is on the face of the pile in your left hand (Illus. 16).

"Here's my lucky card," you declare. Name the card. "If it's to do any good, we'll have to turn it over." Turn it over in place. Close up the cards. Turn the deck face down. The twenty-sixth card from the bottom is now face up in the face-down deck.

Illus. 16

Hand the deck back to Leonard, saying, "Please think of a number from one to ten." Turn away. "Count off that number of cards from the top, and place them in your pocket or hide them somewhere else. I don't want to know your number." Pause. "Now look at the card that lies at that same number from the top and show it around. But make sure to keep it at that same number. For instance, if your number was three, you would look at the third card from the top. Be sure to remember that card because now that's your lucky card."

Turn back to the group. "We have my lucky card turned face up somewhere in the deck. Now let's try my lucky number. I wanted a lucky number that no one else had, so I chose 13. Please deal off 13 cards into a pile." Leonard does so. "Now into another pile, deal as many cards as you want, but make sure you deal past my lucky card, or this trick won't work."

When Leonard finishes, pick up the second pile he dealt and turn it face up. "Take the other pile, Leonard. Let's deal our cards into separate piles. I'll deal mine face up; you deal yours face down. We'll do it together so we match each other card for card. When we come to my face-down card, we'll stop." Immediately after dealing off your face-down card, stop the deal. Turn the card over, saying, "There it is. . .my lucky card." Ask him to name the card he chose. Point to the last card he dealt and ask him to turn it over. "Look at that—there's your lucky card."

MAGIC SPELLS

Simple Speller

The first part of this trick can be done facing the spectators, but I prefer to turn my back. Ask Annette to help by shuffling the deck. Turn away and give the following instructions:

"Annette, look through the deck and find any two spot cards. Place them face up on the table, side by side. Now deal face-down cards on each one so that the total will equal ten. For instance, if you have a 7 face up, you would deal a card face down on it, saying eight. . .deal another, saying nine. . .and a final card, saying ten—a total of ten. Do this for both cards."

Pause.

"Notice the total of the two face-up cards. Deal that many into a separate pile from the top of the deck. Now look at the top card of the deck and show it around. That's your chosen card. Replace it on top of the deck and put the deck on the table. Pick up the pile you counted off, mix it up, and put the cards on top of the deck. You have two small piles left on the table. Turn down the face-up card in each pile. Mix the two piles together and place the cards on top of the deck."

Turn back to the group. Address Annette: "Why have I had you go through all this? Two reasons: So that you would have complete freedom of choice, and so that the position of the card in the deck would be a complete mystery to me. Therefore, we must resort to magic."

Since the trick is completely self-working, you could simply proceed. But it's best to give the spectators something extra to think about. I usually take the pack, give it one "magic riffle," and return it to my helper. All I do is riffle the ends of the deck upwards.

"I'd like you to spell out a sentence," I say, "dealing out one card for each letter. Here's the sentence: 'The next card will be yours.'"

Guide her through it. Naturally, when she finishes the spelling, you have her turn over the next card. That's it all right.

Note

Any 22-letter sentence will work. You can improvise a sentence using the spectator's name, for instance.

Nine to One

This trick was inspired by a Martin Gardner invention and a derivation by Robert Neale.

In your pocket you have a packet of nine cards. The suits are unimportant, so from the face of the packet to the top these are the values: 3, jack, ace, king, 7, 4, 2, jack, 8. Let's assume that you're using blue-backed cards. The sixth card from the bottom, the 4, will be red-backed.

Remove the packet from your pocket and turn it face up. Deal it out in three rows so that, as you look at them, the cards are laid out like this:

```
3  J  A
K  7  4
2  J  8
```

Ask Wayne to help out. "This will be a spelling test, Wayne—but a very easy one. We'll see if you can spell out the names of these cards. On the first letter, touch the card you choose to spell. Then you touch the card next to it or below it for the next letter. And so on. For instance, if you were spelling 'seven,' you might do it like this."

Touch the 7 and spell S-E-V-E-N, touching a different card for each letter in the spelling. You may touch the adjoining card on either side, or you may touch the card immediately above or below it. You may not, however, move diagonally. You may, in fact, go back the way you came and touch cards you've touched previously.

Demonstrate the spelling of seven at least twice. The second time, demonstrate how Wayne might retrace his steps and touch a card more than once.

"You may start on any card, and we'll see how many you can spell."

He spells out a card. Have him hold his finger on the one he lands on. "Let's get rid of the face cards. Which one should we turn down first?" Turn over whichever one he indicates. "This is going to get tough now, because you have to end up on a face-up card. Now turn over the card you landed on and then spell it out the same way as you did the first one. By the way, you can spell on a face-down card; you just can't land on one."

He starts with the card he landed on and spells out its value as he did before. Have him hold his finger on it. "We'd better get rid of another face card. Which one?" He tells you, and you turn it face down. Again he notes the card he landed on, turns it face down, and then spells it out.

"Now we'll get rid of that last face card," you say, turning it face down.

Wayne continues the spelling process until only one card remains face up.

"Congratulations, Wayne. You did it perfectly. Remember now, you had complete freedom of choice as to which cards you would spell and how you would spell them. And there's only one card that you chose not to spell."

Turn the remaining card—the 4—face down in place. The red back stands out among the blue-backed cards. "Well, no wonder. It doesn't fit in with all the rest."

Note

Why does this work? As I indicated, something of a mathematical principle is in operation. Cards can be spelled out in three, four, or five letters. Since some cards are spelled out with an odd number of letters and some with an even number of letters, all one needs to do is to place the cards so that the red-backed card can never be reached by the spelling procedure. The trouble is that three other cards cannot be reached, either. Therefore, place face cards in these positions and eliminate them as the trick proceeds.

Obviously, any three- or five-letter cards can be substituted for the ones I use in the layout.

RED & BLACK

Stop Sign

Roy Walton invented this location trick.

Ask Doug to shuffle the pack and then deal into a face-down pile. He must deal fewer than 26. Secretly keep track of the number he deals. Subtract this number from 27. This is your key number. Suppose he's dealt 18 cards. Subtract 18 from 27, giving you 9. You must remember the number nine.

Tell Doug, "Please pick up the cards you dealt off. Fan through them and secretly count the red cards." When he's done, turn away, and continue: "Set that pile down and pick up the rest of the deck. Now you counted a certain number of red cards. I want you to look at the faces and count to that same number in black cards. For instance, if you counted 12 red cards, you'd count to the twelfth black card from the bottom. That will be your selected card." When he's done, say, "Close up the cards and turn them face down. Place them on top of the pile on the table."

Turn back, pattering, "What we've tried to do is have a card selected completely at random. Now let's see if I can read your thoughts. Pick up the deck and slowly deal the cards, one by one, into a face-up pile. When you come to your card, I want you to think 'stop.' But try not to pause, hesitate, or in any way give away the position of your card. Just continue dealing at the same pace."

As he deals, count the black cards. The card that lies at

your key number (in our example, the ninth black card) is the one he chose. Let him deal a card or two more and then say, "I got a strong impression a moment ago." Push the chosen card out from the others. "Is this your card?"

The One & Only

The original trick is the invention of Karl Fulves. In its effect, it is somewhat similar to "Nine to One," on page 33, but the principle is totally different.

Let's assume you're using a deck with blue backs. You're going to use 16 cards, eight of the black suits and eight of the red suits. The values and the specific suits don't matter. One of the red-suit cards, however, will be from a different deck and will have a red back. Let's say this card is the queen of hearts.

Remove the packet of 16 cards from your pocket and turn it face up. Deal the cards out face up. This is how they'll appear from the spectator's view:

B	R	R	R
R	B	B	B
R	B	QH	R
R	B	B	B

So, for you to deal the packet out in a natural order—left to right, one row below another—the cards must be set up, from the bottom of the packet, like this:

B B B R, R QH B R, B B B R, R R R B

You'll also need a marker of some sort. A mysterious-looking medal or a foreign coin is perfect. Any coin will do, however. Hand the coin to a spectator, saying, "This will aid us in an experiment to determine whether our minds are in tune. If all works out, it might be an example of coincidence. . .or it might be some mysterious form of telepathy. I'll turn my back and give you some instructions. I want you to act on impulse only. Do whatever first occurs to you. If you stop to think, it could conceivably interfere with any possible telepathic waves."

Turn away and give the following instructions, pausing after each:

"Place the coin on any red card—complete freedom of choice."

"Move the coin to the left or the right to the nearest black card; you may choose either left or right. If there's no black card to the left or right, just leave the coin where it is."

"Move the coin either up or down to the nearest red card. Again, you have the choice of going either up or down."

"Move the coin diagonally to the nearest black card."

"Move the coin either down—towards you—or to the right to the nearest red card."

Turn back. The coin should be resting on the queen of hearts. "Let's see if we were able to mentally communicate." Turn over, in place, all of the cards except for the queen of hearts. "All blue backs." Remove the coin from the queen of hearts and turn the card over. It is, of course, the only card with a red back.

LONG-DISTANCE CALLS

Phony Coincidence

By way of preparation, write a column of numbers, from one to 35, on a sheet of paper. Phone Ramona and ask her to get a deck of cards.

"Please give the cards a good shuffle, Ramona. Now it happens that I'm thinking of a particular card. I wonder if you'd choose the same card. Let's find out. Cut off a pile of cards. Set the rest of the deck aside. Now from the top, deal your cards into a face-up pile. Please name each card as you deal it out. Keep going until you finish the pile you cut off."

As Ramona names each card, jot down that number next to the appropriate number on your sheet. (Use this shorthand: For 9 of clubs, 9C; for queens of spades, QS; for ace of hearts, AH, etc.)

When Ramona finishes naming the cards, say, "That's amazing! My card is in that group."

Your key numbers are 1, 2, 4, 8, 16, 32. Note how many cards are in Ramona's pile. Subtract from this the next-lower key number. Suppose the pile contained 23 cards. Subtract the next-lower key number, which is 16. Twenty-three minus 16 is 7. Double the result, which gives you 14. Look at your sheet. The card at number 14 will be the one you're thinking of.

Say to Ramona, "Pick up your pile and turn the cards face down. Now deal the top card onto the deck and put the next one on the bottom of your pile. Put the next one on top of the deck and the next one on the bottom of your pile. Keep doing this until you have only one card left."

When she's done, say, "The card I was thinking of was. . ." Name the card you noted at number 14. Ask, "What's your card?" It's the same, of course.

A brief review of the latter part of the trick: Your helper has finished listing her cards. You note the number in the pile. Suppose the total is 14. You subtract from this the next-lower key number, which is 8. Fourteen minus 8 is six. You double 6, giving you 12. The card you noted at number 12 will be the one your helper will end up with.

Are You There?

Have a pencil and paper ready. Phone a friend and ask him to get out a deck of cards. Give him the following directions:

"Shuffle the deck. Look at the bottom card and remember it. Count onto the table from the top of the deck a number equal to the value of the card you looked at. A jack counts as 11, a queen 12, and a king 13. Now place the rest of the deck on top of those cards."

When he's done, say, "Now name the cards, starting with the top card of the deck and working on down." After he names the first card, say, "Stop! I forgot something. Put that card back on top. I wanted you to cut the cards first. Cut off about half the cards and place the other half on top."

But make sure you jot down the name of the card he called out. This is your key card. After he cuts the cards, say, "Now please name the cards, starting with the top card."

As he names the cards, jot down their names, using this shorthand: AC, 9H, 2D, etc. Stop writing when the spectator calls the name of the key card. Suppose that card were the 9 of diamonds. These might be the last 15 cards you jotted down:

5D 2H 7H 10H 5H 9H JS 5C AC KD JC 8H 7S 4D 9D
13 12 11 10 9 8 7 6 5 4 3 2 1 — —

Now number the cards as above. Don't put a number under your key card, nor under the card named before it.

When a number corresponds to the value of a listed card, that's the chosen card. In the example above, the chosen card is the 10 of hearts. If there are two possibilities, eliminate one by naming the suit or value of one of the cards. For instance, you might say, "I get a strong feeling that your card is a club." If your assistant agrees, you have the right card. If you're wrong, name the other possibility.

Something to Sniff At

As far as I know, the original telephone trick was called The Wizard. Spread out the cards face up and have someone push out a card. Then dial "The Wizard," actually a confederate. When your friend answers the phone, ask, "Is The Wizard there?" Immediately the confederate begins naming the suits. Upon hearing the correct suit, you say, "Hello." Your confederate now knows the suit of the chosen card. She immediately begins naming the values, like this, "Ace, king, queen, jack, 10," etc. When she names the proper value, say, "Here," and hand the phone to the person who chose the card. The Wizard immediately tells him the name of his card.

Here we have an extremely subtle adaptation of the same trick. Again, the deck is spread out face up and a spectator pushes out a card. Dial the number of your confederate. When she answers, clear your throat. As before, she begins naming the suits. When she hits the correct suit, you sniff. She names the values. When she hits the right value, you again sniff.

Hand the phone to the spectator. Whisper to him, "Ask for your card any way you want to." When the spectator says "Hello," your confederate says, "Hello, hello. Who's calling, please? Hello." This, of course, creates the illusion that she's just answered the phone.

The spectator asks for the name of his card and is given the correct answer.

SPECIAL ARRANGEMENTS

Easy Opener

Jay Ose often used this opening trick; I've made a few minor changes.

Remove the four aces from the deck. The ace of hearts goes on top of the deck, and the ace of diamonds goes on the bottom. The third card from the top is the ace of clubs, and the fourth card from the top is the ace of spades. Place the deck in its card case.

In performance, get a volunteer—Susie, for instance. Remove the deck from its case and set the case aside. Set the deck on the table. Make sure no one gets a peek at the bottom card.

"Susie, I'd like you to think of an ace—A-C-E, ace. It could be your favorite ace, or one you don't care for at all. Do you have an ace in mind? What is it?"

She names the ace. Suppose she names the ace of hearts. Say, "Put your hand on top of the deck and say, 'I want the top card to be the ace of hearts.'" She does so. Have her lift her hand. Turn over the top card, showing that her wish has come true.

Suppose she names the ace of diamonds. Say, "Put your hand on top of the deck and say, 'I want the bottom card to be the ace of diamonds.'" She removes her hand and you turn the deck over, showing the bottom card. Make sure that you don't inadvertently show the top card as well.

Suppose she names the ace of clubs or the ace of spades. Say, "As I said, 'Ace, A-C-E.'" Pick up the deck. Spell out A-C-E, dealing one card from the top into a pile for each letter. If she named the ace of clubs, turn over the last card you dealt. If she named the ace of spades, turn over the current top card of the deck.

In all instances, gather up the cards and give them a good shuffle, destroying all the evidence. As you do so, patter about how incredible it is that she should have thought of that very ace. Go right into your next trick.

It's In Your Hands

The spectator handles the cards throughout an "impossible" location of a chosen card.

In preparation, remove all the clubs from the deck. From top to bottom, arrange them in this order:

10 9 8 7 6 5 4 3 2 A K Q J

The stack goes on the bottom of the deck, making the jack of clubs the bottom card.

In performance, set the deck face down on the table. Ask Bert to cut off a portion and shuffle it. Make sure he doesn't cut into your stack. "Replace the packet on top of the deck, please. Then take the top card, show it around, and replace it on the top."

When Bert's done, have him give the pack a complete cut. He, or someone else, gives the deck another complete cut.

Say, "Let's try something different. Turn the deck face up and give the cards a complete cut."

Have various spectators continue cutting the cards until a club shows up on the face of the deck. At this point, say, "That should be enough. The cards should be sufficiently mixed. Turn the deck face down, please."

You now know the position of the chosen card from the top. How? You add 3 to the value of the bottom card. Suppose a spectator has cut the 6 of clubs to the bottom. Add 3 to 6, getting 9. The chosen card is ninth from the top. The ace is figured as one.

The obvious exception is when the jack, queen, or king

of clubs is cut to the face of the deck. Just consider the jack as one, the queen as two, and the king as three—which should be easy to remember. So if the jack appears on the bottom, the chosen card will be on top; if the queen is on the bottom, the chosen card will be second from the top; and if it's the king, the chosen card will be third from the top.

As before, suppose the 6 of clubs was on the bottom. The deck is now face down on the table, and you know the chosen card is ninth from the top.

Harry Lorayne suggested this procedure: Have the spectator place his hand on the deck. Say, "Your card is forty-first from the top, so please push down on the deck. Good! It's now twenty-fifth from the top. Push down a little harder. Hold it, hold it! You now have it ninth from the top. Any more pushing and you might push it out of the deck altogether. Let's check that ninth card and see if I'm right."

Have the spectator deal off nine cards into a pile. Ask him to name his card and then to turn over the last one dealt.

Note

In the original version of this trick, the cards were stacked on the bottom in their natural order. This could give the trick away. A five shows up on the bottom, and the chosen card is five from the top. Not good.

Cutting the Aces

Wally Wilson dazzled me with this trick. I have no idea who originated the effect, which is a clever adaptation of an old principle.

A simple setup is necessary. Collect the four aces and arrange them, along with two other cards, like this: Place an ace face up on the table. On top of this place another ace face up. The next card—any card but an ace—is also face up. On this place any card but an ace face down. And, on top of all, two face-down aces. So, from the top down, you have three face-down cards (ace, ace, any card), fol-

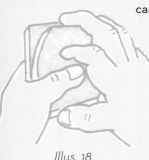

Illus. 17

Two Aces

lowed by three face-up cards (any card, ace, ace) (Illus. 17). Place the whole stack on top of the deck.

Ready? Ask a spectator to help you. "As I riffle these cards, please stick your finger in wherever you wish." Hold the deck in the dealing position in your left hand. With your right fingers, riffle the outer end of the deck from the bottom up, going as slowly as you can (Illus. 18). After the spectator inserts his fin-

Illus. 18

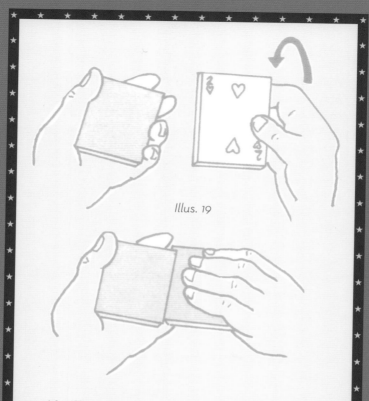

Illus. 19

ger, lift off the upper portion with your right hand, allowing withdrawal of his finger. Turn this packet over sideways and place it face up onto the cards in your left hand, saying, "We'll mark the exact spot you chose."

Even up all the cards. Ask: "And where's the card you selected?" Fan through the pack to the first face-down card. Lift the face-up cards with your right hand. With your left thumb, push off the first face-down card so that it drops to the table, still face down.

Turn over the cards in your right hand end for end and place them beneath those in your left hand (Illus. 19).

Repeat the entire maneuver, starting with riffling the outer ends of the cards for the insertion of the spectator's finger. The business is performed four times in all.

At the end, you say, "Let's see which cards you selected." Turn the aces face up one by one.

Note

You'll end up with a face-up card in the deck. If you don't have an opportunity to secretly turn the card over, simply proceed with other tricks. What with various spectators shuffling the deck, it's not unusual that a card should turn out to be face up. When it's noticed, simply say, "No wonder I'm having so much trouble. We've got a face-up card here." Then turn the card over.

"Guts" Poker

U. F. Grant developed a brief poker demonstration. The demonstration should be done while seated at a table.

To start, you must have the four aces on top of the deck. Casually give the deck a few riffle-shuffles, keeping the four aces on top.

Explain, "Card sharps usually win, not by cheating, but because they know the odds. Sometimes they resort to cheating. But I've discovered that you don't have to know the odds and you don't have to cheat—*if* you're very lucky. And I happen to be very lucky. Let me demonstrate."

Ask Woody, who's seated opposite you, to help out. Set the deck down and ask the person seated to your right to cut the cards. After he picks a packet from the top, pick up the lower portion and begin dealing. This is a fairly normal procedure in informal games. The person who cut the cards will place his portion on the table.

Deal two poker hands in the normal manner—one to Woody and one to yourself. "This will be a wide-open game," you say. "You may draw as many cards as you want. But not more than five. . .if you don't mind."

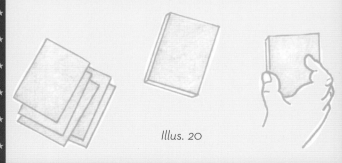

Illus. 20

You're still holding the packet you dealt from. "How many cards do you want?" He tosses some cards aside, and you deal him the same number. Then casually set the remaining cards down *to the right* of the other packet on the table (Illus. 20). Pick up your hand and study it, murmuring something like, "I seem to have run out of luck. This is the worst hand I've *ever* held." The point is to kill a little time, giving onlookers a chance to forget which packet is which. Finally discard four cards from your hand. "I guess I'll take four."

Pick up the pile which was originally the top section and deal yourself four cards—the aces, of course. Place the remaining cards on top of the packet on the table.

Do some imaginary betting with Woody, then ask him to show his hand. "As I mentioned, you don't have to be skillful—if you're lucky."

Turn over your cards one at a time.

ALL IN THE MIND

You Might Wonder

You might wonder why a trick this simple would work. After the deck is shuffled by a spectator, Ernie, take the cards back. Comment that you need a prediction card as you fan through the deck, faces towards yourself. At first, fan rapidly through the cards, noting the top card. Then fan through more slowly, looking for the mate to the top card—the one that matches it in color and value. Remove that card and set it aside, face down, announcing that it's your prediction.

Hand the deck face down to Ernie, saying, "Please deal the cards one at a time into a face-down pile." After he's dealt 15 cards or so, say, "You may stop any time you wish." When he stops, take the remainder of the cards from him and set them aside.

Tell him, "Pick up the pile you dealt and turn it face up. Now deal those into a face-up pile and stop whenever you wish." Again, when he stops, take the cards remaining in his hand and set them aside. Say, "Pick up the pile, turn it face down, and deal as many as you wish."

He stops; you take the remaining cards and set them aside. He continues, alternately dealing from a face-up packet and a face-down packet, until only one card remains. Take this card and set it next to your prediction card. If the card is face up, simply turn over your prediction card, showing the match. If the card is face down, turn over the two cards simultaneously.

Note

Make sure that the top card isn't an obvious one, like an ace or face card. On every other deal, the "chosen" card is briefly displayed, so it should be a spot card, which is unlikely to be noted. If the top card is an ace or face card, have a spectator give the cards an additional shuffle.

Lie Like a Rug

Jack Vosburgh invented this trick.

Before you begin, sneak a peek at the top card of the deck. Then you'll need the assistance of three spectators.

Set the deck on the table and ask one of the spectators to cut the cards into three piles. Each of the spectators now chooses a pile and takes the top card from it. Your job is to note which of the three takes the card that you know.

Explain, "This is an informal lie detector test. Over the years I've acquired the ability to tell if someone is lying. Let's test it out. In a moment, I'd like the three of you to decide which one of you will tell the truth about the card he selected. So one of you will be a truth-teller. The other two should name each other's card."

Make sure all is understood, then turn away while the three make their decision. When you turn back, ask each spectator in turn which card he took. Then point to one spectator, saying, "You're lying." Point to a second spectator and repeat the accusation. Point to the third spectator, saying, "Congratulations! You are a truth-teller."

How do you know? Simple. If the person who took the card you peeked at names that card, the other two are liars. If he names some other card, then he is one of the liars; the other liar is the one who names the card you peeked at.

Perfectly Mental

In many respects, this trick is a perfect demonstration of mind reading. A card is freely chosen and returned to the deck. The spectator immediately shuffles the deck. Nevertheless, the mentalist finds the card.

Every so often, the trick will misfire. If there is such a thing as telepathy, isn't it logical that occasionally the mentalist will get the wrong signal?

Start by getting a peek at the bottom card. This is your key card. You may give the pack a riffle shuffle, keeping the card on the bottom. Set the deck on the table and ask Leah to cut off a portion of the cards and set them on the table. Say, "Please take the card you cut to and show it around, but don't let me get a look at it." When she's done, point to the portion she cut off, saying, "Replace your card here and then put the rest of the deck on top." After she does so, say, "Now give the cards a good shuffle."

If she gives the deck one shuffle, say, "And another." Chances are, however, she'll give the cards two or three shuffles on her own. It doesn't matter whether she gives the pack riffle-shuffles, overhand shuffles, or a combination.

Take back the deck, saying, "I'd like you all to mentally picture the chosen card. Maybe this will help me discover which one it is." With an expression of deep concentration, fan through the cards, faces towards yourself. Watch for your key card. The one just preceding it is probably the chosen card. Tentatively pull this card from the deck, shaking your head. "I don't get strong vibrations, but this might be your card." Set the card face down on the table. Ask Leah to name her selection. If you get it right, nod, and turn the card over. If not, replace the card in the deck, saying, "Yes, I was afraid of that." Follow up with a sure-fire mental trick.

Notes

It's possible that the chosen card could be separated from your key card by one, two, or three cards. Some prefer asking probing questions to see if this is what's happened. When this is the case, the mentalist is often able to come up with the chosen card—eventually. I prefer the straightforward method, even though there's a minor risk of failure.

You can make this trick almost a certainty by using *two* easily remembered key cards, like the two black aces. Beforehand, for example, you might place the ace of clubs on top of the deck and the ace of spades on the bottom. Proceed as described above.

When you fan through the deck and find a single card between the two aces, you can be quite confident that's the one chosen. But suppose the black aces are separated. In all likelihood, the chosen card is the one preceding the ace of spades or the one after the ace of clubs. To discover which, ask a question to distinguish the two possibilities, like, "Was it a face card?" or "Was it a red card?" or "Did it have a very low value?"

As with the version using one key card, reveal your choice in a very tentative manner, leaving yourself an excuse for a possible failure.

The Bamboozler

Get a peek at the top card of the deck. Give the cards a riffle-shuffle, keeping it on top. Set the deck down on the table. Ask Megan to cut off a pile, gesturing to show that she is to place the top portion nearer herself. Tap the card which she cut to, saying, "This card will tell me. . ." Point to the top card of the pile nearer her, continuing, ". . .what that card is."

Lift off the card she cut to, look at it, remember it, and replace it. Make sure no one else can see its face. "Your card is—" Name the card you peeked at originally. Have her turn the card over. You're right, of course. Toss this card aside face up.

Place the packet nearer you on top of the other packet. Once more you know the top card of the deck and are ready for a repeat. But not until you blather for a moment.

"That always seems to work the first time I try it," you might say, "but the second time is almost impossible. But I have to try; otherwise, you might think it was mere coincidence."

Repeat the trick, again discarding the named card face up. Replace your pile on top of Megan's. Again you know the top card.

"This last time I'm going to attempt something even more difficult. I'm going to name both cards," you say.

Suppose the card now on top of the deck is the ace of clubs. Megan again cuts off a pile. Tap the card she cut to, saying, "This is the ace of clubs." Lift off the card and look at it. Suppose it's the 3 of hearts. Nod your head and say, "Good."

Tap the top card of Megan's pile. "And this is the 3 of hearts." Lift the card off and hold it next to the actual 3 of hearts, making sure no one can see the faces of the cards (Illus. 21).

Illus. 21

"Oh-oh!" You appear disappointed as you see what the second card is. "I can't believe this."

Pause, shaking your head. "Ace of clubs and 3 of hearts." Take one of the cards into your right hand. Turn your hands over and simultaneously drop the two cards face up onto the table. This maneuver masks their original position in your hand.

Note

This trick is definitely a "quickie;" don't dawdle.

The Hocus-Pocus Pairs

Remove from the deck all aces, kings, queens, jacks, and tens, placing the cards face up in a neat pile on the table. But don't remove the cards in their natural order. You want to create the notion that the selection is random. You might, for example, remove the cards in this order: 10, queen, ace, jack, and king. Remove another set of five cards to match these exactly. In other words, take out another 10, queen, ace, jack, and king. These are placed, one at a time, on top of the first set. When the packet is turned face down, the cards will be, from the top down, 10, queen, ace, jack, king, 10, queen, ace, jack, and king.

While doing this, explain, "I need fairly high cards for this experiment. Somehow or other, it always seems to work better with high cards. Maybe higher cards have more power."

Pick up the packet and turn it face down. Hold the cards in your left hand as though about to perform an overhand shuffle (Illus. 22). Lift some cards from the bottom with your right hand and drop these on top. Do this several times rapidly, as though shuffling. Actually, you're merely giving the packet complete cuts. The action should be performed casually as you continue chatting. Set the packet on the table and have spectators give it several complete cuts.

Illus. 78

"We have ten cards here." Deal five cards into a pile, saying, "One, two, three, four, five." Fan out the remaining cards, saying, "And five more." Close up the fan and place this pile next to the other. You now have two piles on the table. One pile is in reverse order to the other. The first pile, for instance, might be in this order: ace, jack, king, 10, and queen. If so, the second pile will be in this order: queen, 10, king, jack, and ace.

Request Rosemary's help. "What brings about a miraculous result?" you ask. "The occult? Coincidence? We seldom know. Let's eliminate all but two cards and see if these two will match. We'll start by giving you a choice of two words which might bring about a miraculous result. An astonishing result might be caused by telepathy or luck. Choose one of those: telepathy or luck."

Rosemary selects one of the words.

Ask her: "Pick up either pile and spell that word, transferring one card from the top to the bottom for each letter in the spelling. You need not stick with one pile. You can spell a few from one and then a few from the other—any way you want to do it—just so you spell the word correctly."

When she's done, take the top card from each pile. Put them together and set them aside face down. "There. We've eliminated one pair. Now you have another choice to make. A miracle could be brought about through ESP or fortune. Choose one of those please."

After she chooses, have her spell out her choice, transferring cards from top to bottom, just as she did before. Again make it clear that she may switch piles at random as she does the spelling. When she finishes, set the top card of each pile aside as a pair, just as before. Say, "Another pair eliminated."

"You're now down to three cards in each pile. Time for another choice. An apparent miracle might be caused by magic or by accident. Choose either magic or accident. Choose one and spell it out."

As before, when Rosemary finishes, set the top two cards aside as a pair.

"And again a choice. Is a miraculous result brought about by sorcery or skill? Please pick one and spell it out."

When she finishes, take the top two cards and set them aside as a pair, saying, "So we've eliminated the last pair. Only two cards are left. You've had several choices in eliminating the various pairs. Wouldn't it be an amazing coincidence if these two cards should match?"

Turn the two cards over, showing the match. Pause for a moment, as though through with the trick. "That may be coincidence, Rosemary, but let's see if you really have the power."

Turn over each of the other pairs, showing the other four matches.

Notes

For the trick to work, the exact words must be used each time. You might choose to carry a calling card on which you have the four pairs of words listed. At the appropriate time, take out the calling card, saying, "This experiment won't work unless we use the appropriate magical words." I prefer to have the "magical words" memorized.

INDEX